THE MOTHER HOUSE

THE MOTHER HOUSE

EILÉAN NÍ CHUILLEANÁIN

WAKE FOREST

UNIVERSITY PRESS

For permission, write to

Wake Forest University Press

Post Office Box 7333

Winston-Salem, NC 27109

wfupress.wfu.edu

wfupress@wfu.edu

ISBN 978-1-930630-92-5 (paperback)

Library of Congress Control Number: 2019950176

Designed and typeset by Crisis

Publication of this book was generously

supported by the Boyle Family Fund.

THE MOTHER HOUSE

AN IMPERFECT ENCLOSURE

FOR NANO NAGLE, 1718−84

She was out in all weathers.
She was tired, someone gave her
a chair in a shop. Rested
and then away, in the street, on the move.

The house she built first, giving
on the street—could she close up
doors and windows on that side?
It would be noticed as a convent.

She asked to be buried in
the common cemetery.
They broke through the wall
of the nuns' graveyard

and slipped her coffin inside.
But she would not stay,
so they built her a stone tomb
nearer to Cove Lane

and opened a latch at one end
so hands can touch the coffin.

SHE WAS AT THE HAYMAKING

She was down in the small field
turning the last swaths of hay
on the slope facing the river mouth

(each time she came back up
she saw the wave so gently courting
the land, with shallow pushes

and the curved edge of the tide
making its way upstream)
she was alone in the field—

they were up in the house with Mary
whose bag was packed, waiting for the car
to bring her on the first stage,

the start of her long voyage
away to the far shores
of America and the novitiate.

She worked on with the rake
thinking of the rolling wave,
an eye watching for the car.

When she heard it on the road
she brought the rake up with her
on the steep path to the house.

They were all there in the parlor,
Mary sitting in the middle,
her face amazed. "I can't go."

"Now that it's time, I can't go."
Her parents said nothing. Her sister
had come to bid her goodbye,

now she said, "So I'll go."
She shook a small bit of hay
out of her hair. She washed her hands,

she took up the bag and went off with the driver
to a house full of rules—so far away
that when she wrote to say she was happy

the letter took three weeks crossing the sea.

A JOURNEY

I went driving through the countries
where I could read the names,
the posters outside cinemas,
the leaflets in the churches;

the scripts began to slow me down
after the mountain border climb
and beyond the roadblock I could see
only the shapes: the shed end

and the parked van, and the slow-
motion shadow of somebody
at the edge of the road. I looked
again at the deep wound in my arm;

it was all cleaned and covered up,
so as not to frighten the children.

THE UNRECONCILE

The numbers work their tricks, dividing and stacking in columns
that shake when a draft from an open diary or
an old account-book slips its blade in between:
nineteen-sixty-seven, seventy, seventy-one, seventy-eight,

eighty-three, eighty-four, eighty-nine, two thousand and nine.
A boy fretting on the bus to school is one.
A girl on the train from Fishguard to Oxford is one.
A woman in London queuing in Outpatients is still one.

Exile-sex-death: just as Charles Baudelaire saw the swan
on the building site in Paris, gray webbed feet on the dry
stones, his open beak, stretched neck, in the pose Ovid
explains is peculiar to human beings, and he thought

about Andromache's tears, the little river she invented,
about the consumptive African woman tramping the foggy street,
he thought of slender orphans withering like flowers,
of the defeated, of stranded sailors, and so on—

nothing can shift the weight, the hundred stones in the schoolyard
are founded on deeper buried stones, a hundred
men and women are crying in underground hospital carparks—
no river and no rain can wash any of this away.

LOVE

The view from the train is better than a dream.
A man is gazing down his lines of beetroot,
A lone tractor waits at the level crossing,
one light glowing although it's not quite dark.
A doll has fallen into the gloom of the hedge,
her frilly skirt still white. Walls come closer,
lights on Clara station cast their orange trawl.
Beyond its margin, the engines
vibrate in the carpark, harmonizing the hum of love.

A newspaper spread on a dashboard
catches the last light from an office window;
a parent's overcoated shape is reading,
waiting for the noisy gang that clings
by the doors with their luggage while
the wheels are slowing and finally slide and stand.

KILMAINHAM

Tell me he said how you managed to break out of my jail
so that I can build a better one that will not fail.

So I explained about the whistle and the gin,
the special shoes and so forth, and I threw in

the ropes made out of blankets, the false handcuffs, the vitriol,
the cunning tailored loose-cut trousers, the tobacco-pipe, and all

to distract him from the innocent who passed down the high wall
at my side, who is wandering the world now
transparent as the ocean, direct as the shallow flow
of tides over stones, will he make it home, or must he fall.

ON THE MOVE

ARTHUR MAXIMILIAN WOODS, AUGUST 2015

The path turns right, and turns again where the sheep
spotted a sweeter tuft of grass—
it halts by bridges, under trees, it keeps going—
Arthur is ready to follow, he stands
barefoot on the cool grass. Go on, Arthur,
follow the path, walk on the grass not the gravel, until
when you look back the house has disappeared.

The window seems quite plain while he is out of view
and when he surfaces again our sight
fills up like a full glass. It's the trick of a road
emptying itself, a stage where someone's
hidden by flat forest scenery, and when the cue arrives
he passes along remote and small
until turning to meet us again, making for home—

loaded, we'll see, when he empties his pockets,
with mountains, friends, pine cones, clouds and such stuff.

RESEMBLANCES

My mother nodding down at me from her portrait
in the hall never looked so still in her lifetime,
only when she sat for Edward McGuire
who loaded her with a black cloak from Kinsale.
She does look like herself though,
as Adam looked like God
but also looked like Eve.
Do I look like her? I am older
now, than her age when she died.

I head upstairs and see myself,
and see my room, the books
on their shelves, all the wrong way round,
rearranged in the beveled glass of my aunt's
complicated sideboard, which sits
across the landing from the study door.
Like everything that I deal with now the room
has a double, a frill of light surrounding it.

When I kill the landing light,
the books are still present for a moment
in the glow from the laptop screen facing the shelves,
their new regime still briefly stamped
in the memory of mercury and glass.

THE BLIND

i

One broken slat pulled from the blind
shows only a slice: the marbled clouds,
a world of bright sky stretching.

But she can't look out. The news,
a thread that crawls and winds, drags her
into the dark well

that widens then pulls tighter:
what is down there is heavy
and it is true. It pulls on her skin.

All of her is in here,
it is all in the rule, every stitch that
she is wearing, every minute

in the table of the day, each
close-packed piece of type
that printed her instructions.

ii

After all, she looks out, a slight turn
and her cheek is against the blind, she sees
the boats are coming home, their path

curved and yielding to the current;
they scatter and cluster again, to follow
into the small harbor, one by one;

when the last one has passed under the tower
the light of evening is offered—
like a bowl that is offered, held in both hands,
the milk-white light fills
the whole wide empty bay.

ALLOW PLENTY OF TIME

Can I pause, will there be time to pause
along the way, how long will it last,
that spell when I can't move and can't turn a page,

before facing the road? The Russians in *War and Peace*
before the failed abduction, the smokers
outside the slow café, watching

a slow goods train stretching itself out—
they all do it naturally and don't need
a tap on the glass or a church bell

to make them shiver and then
slowly begin again

THE CAT DINNER

We knew they were there, their flattened black masks,
and that when they withdrew into lunar shadow
there would be no witness, a cobwebby silence.

Lips open but speech fails, round the half-cleared table,
sitting there, but strangers, our fussy notes shuffled,
lying at random. We made the long journey

to deliver the gesture, but who has noticed us?
—like the food left outside for visiting spirits
which is gone next morning, but did the cats eat it?

A MAP OF CONVENTS

FOR MARGARET MACCURTAIN

Cove Lane

. . . and I took in children by degrees, not to make any
noise about it in the beginning. In about nine months
I had about two hundred children. —Nano Nagle

Here is the map, with the underground streams,
the vessels that shrug at their tether, the walled islands,
and the fine gardens. There was another map,
of a different place, in her head; she told nobody.

Nothing gave her away, not her clothes,
or the clothes of her company, secular and plain,
or the cabin in the southwest corner
where now the playing-field is hard ground.

It was poor like the shacks and cellars
piled together in the laneways
that sloped up from the South Channel.
The map of the city never showed
those children swiftly assembling
into a parliament of girls and boys.

Work

Try it again, says the voice. After that
a tinkling, the last piano lesson
joins up with the mutter of Latin,
the scholarship class getting a final trot
through the metrics of Horace's *Odes*—
and soon it will be all stillness indoors.

Now silence is waiting, a music from under the floor
too deep to be heard, a procession pacing
with tall faded banners that sway and swallow
the laneways' clatter and the brewery smell.
It flows like a tide, it encloses our evening.
It's as if we grew gills like fish to breathe it in deeply.

Inside the House

She crossed the footbridge, the bell
was ringing from the chapel, they were there
expecting her. In she went,
inside, like breathing, her quest
for the kernel, the seed
that might burst and make a way
of release for her, escape—
even if its hiding place was a shell,
even if it had to be hidden
like the fragile yolk that held the giant's life:

she plumbed the basement and searched inside the chimneys.

She laughed telling the story.
O, you'd do that, she said,
we couldn't have a man inside the door.
The kitchen chimney
and I loved it,
well I remember
the old days, you'd be
black all over after it.

Chapel, 2014

When the rubble is piled in the chancel,
when the eye goes astray
in confusion and the light
entering by the usual window
pauses, at a loss, failing,
missing the usual gleam,
even their shadow scatters
here where they were gathered
in their full bodily presence,

but this is a house of levels
in a city of ridged hills—
the brothers asleep in the crypt
going on two centuries now,
the parlor down at street level
where the girls came for their lesson
still furnished. Empty upstairs the rooms
of those who were absent with permission,
where they studied, where they wept.

When the invaders rifled the convents
they brought these trophies away
and the curious may visit them, here
in the New Wing. Not only St. Catherine
in crimson and pale blue, St. Peter Martyr,
his head cloven, St. Agatha,
St. Margaret with her dragon, but then,
at the side, in the little room,
there is just a scant collection
of empty frames, polished, ornate—
the visitors glance in at them
and pass along, puzzled by the display,
these flourished shapes enclosing
only the wall hanging, dark damask.

I might move on to the long gallery
where the domestic scenery
displays itself at its best,
blond headed families grouped and mingling,
some out of doors, their tall trees shading them,
dandling their tailored sleeves—

but I stay for now, alone

with the frames, their gilded spirals

half shaped like the ring made

by fingers and thumbs of both hands,

their dark-stained quotes, twisted,

curved like the martyr's ribs; like ivy

they shine, they clasp, but it's emptiness

embraced. The scenes (imagine

a triumph with captives, or a judgment

with pillars and guards all ready)—

the scenes are all missing, though the guarded ovals

bleed and reek, the sliced poplar

shifts like a hand mirror offering

a better view of what stank worse

than even the painters could tolerate

in the days when the authorities

advised them to be at their windows

to observe executions, to capture

the reality, to get it right.

THE SMALL MUSEUM

Enormous in the low crypt
(and even taller winged attendants
are offstage pressing to get inside)
the alien vested saints have
waited to manifest, they pounce
and lift up the despicable body,
they place it at the center, the point
where order meets disaster.

We need to be here, our signatures
(which not many will read) must populate
the lower margin, while
on an upper floor of the universe
the man, gigantic and bare, embraces light,
seeks brighter light, ignores the mob
as if he had met us in his own house,
naked at dawn, and we shrink seeing him
since the rising sun and shadows make him
tall as the judge on the day of anger.

SISTER MARINA

"Was there no drama in their lives?"
Once, it was almost Passiontide
and in Lent of course no letters arrived—
people knew better than to write.
So, when a letter landed postmarked Lancaster
for Sister Marina, Reverend Mother
opened and read it and went to find her
just leaving an empty classroom. She closed the door
and handed over the letter. Reverend Mother
was by two years the younger;
now for the first time in her life she saw
a face dragged backwards, dragged down, and how
pain and fear come first, and only about
two seconds later the beginning of thought
weighing down on the heart. She saw the brother's wife,
the brother grim-faced as ever, the sick child
as they printed on the other woman's mind,
as plainly as if a light had flickered
and lit them up in a screened picture.
Nothing that happened after so clearly displayed
how the body is all summed up in a face,
in a flaw—how knowledge travels all the way
down through a body and burns into the floor.
That was drama, she thinks, and hopes for no more.

TO THE MOTHER HOUSE

i

The tender heaved on its way across,
the liner floated grand in the harbor, and the girls
afraid of looking back picked out a porthole
and stared and waited for this parting to be over.

There was a war coming, there was work. The young ones
would never see a soldier, only smile
at meager faces in the alpine sanatorium.
They nursed the miners hammered in the pit,
learning their obstinate love, meeting the mistress
who came after a death with a cushion
to go in the coffin, embroidered with *Bébé*.
The older nun lived through Belsen, sent there
after hiding a crashed airman in the laundry.

ii

Sister Clara, Sister Antony, meeting a niece
in the quiet convent garden in Desvres,
are overheard reminiscing, always in French,

about their first convent on the hill in Cork
and its precious holdings, the Penal Chalice,
the letters from an Italian priest (it's hoped
soon to be beatified), the foundress's diaries,

and all that was sent from the mother house: wine and brandy,
lace, the little medals blessed and certified
in Rome, in the Holy Year. A relic of the True Cross
in its gold box, a fine linen alb embroidered
in Portugal by a novice. Marble for the shrine.

The marble is there still, under the altar.
The mule-driver's curses, the rattling ass and cart
leave no sign on the stone; it sucks in meaning.

Marble is perfect, how it shows the bones
inside the skin, the folds in the light shroud,
and the trailing strands of hair.

WORK

The oldest of all the sisters has to string
little pink beads on the edges of *Agnus Deis*.
She has a basket of the silk badges
and she gets through the heap while she thinks
about prayers and her life. But can she be sure?
What did the sister say only just now,

I hadn't felt that way since ... 1946 ...
and wasn't it later than that, the move
to this house from the old convent?
If she wasn't so stiff she would walk herself,
leaning on her stick up as far as the graveyard,
and check the dates on all of the early crosses.

FOR JAMES CONNOLLY

i

When I think of all the false beginnings . . .
The man was a pair of hands,
the woman another pair, to be had more cheaply,
the wind blew, the children were thirsty—

when he passed by the factory door he saw them,
they were moving and then waiting, as many
as the souls that crowded by Dante's boat

that never settled in the water—
what weight to ballast that ferry?
They are there now, as many

as the souls blown by the winds of their desire,
the airs of love, not one of them weighing
one ounce against the tornado

that lifts the lids off houses, that spies
where they crouch together inside
until the wind sucks them out.

It is only wind, but what braced muscle, what earthed foot
can stand against it, what voice so loud
as to be heard shouting *Enough?*

ii

He had driven the horse in the rubbish cart, he knew
the strength in the neck under the swishing mane,
he knew how to tell her to turn, to back or stand.

He knew where the wind hailed from, he studied
its language, it blew in spite of him.
He got tired waiting for the wind to change,

as we are exhausted waiting for that change,
for the voices to shout *Enough*, for the hands
that can swing the big lever and send the engine rolling

away to the place I saw through the gap in the bone
where there was a painted house, fiddling and the young people
dancing on the shore, and the Old Man of the Sea

had been sunk in the wide calm sea.

iii

The sea moves under the wind and shows nothing—
not where to begin. But look for the moment
just before the wave of change crashes and

goes into reverse. Remember the daft beginnings
of a fatal century and their sad endings, but let's not
hold back our hand from the lever. Remember James Connolly,

who put his hand to the work, who saw suddenly
how his life would end, and was content because
men and women would succeed him, and his testament

was there, he trusted them. It was not a bargain:
in 1916 the printer locked the forme,
he set it in print, the scribes can't alter an iota

—then the reader comes, and it flowers again, like a painted room.

THE LIGHT

FOR DAMHNAIT NÍ RÍORDÁIN

Come out, I say, and you all come to the light.
I look for her, she's there,
the sunlight glancing up from the shining leaves
wavers on her face
as she consults the rose bush, the light moving
in slow time with her hair.

At the end of the garden where the tall trees shivered
the river was in spate.
We walked down there at dawn to get rid of the noise
of the night's debate,
leaving the table with the bottles and empty glasses,
Socrates and his fate

in *Phaedo,* in the Great Books of the World edition
on thin Bible paper
laid open, we left them to look at the river rushing
down to Askeaton,
the tall Desmond castle, the friary beyond the bridge,
in their desolation.

When we turned back, to wash the glasses and arrange
the room before her parents
rose up, she stopped to consult the rose bush, the risen sun
blazed in its ranges;
her face shone green in the glancing light, I remember
across all the changes—

and that they had arrived in the dark, the small shy moths
lined up, wings packed tight,
crowded under the lamp that still shone emptily
recalling the hours of night.

CARR'S LANE

You can see the tall front door
but don't expect to be admitted.
On your left is Carr's Lane,
at the corner a newspaper shop;

up the lane a doorway, steps
worn pale by rain and people climbing,
unlocked at the agreed time
on quiet days for callers they know.

Scholars disagree about
Carr's Lane, is it *cart's lane* corrupted?
Or was there a prosperous
local merchant family called Carr?

They could have grown rich selling
butter to the transatlantic trade
or beef abroad. If their books
gave their story those have all been cleared.

The dealer came one Monday
early, the shelves were bare before noon,
the library is closed off—
dangerous, woodworm in the floorboards.

MARIA EDGEWORTH IN 1847

*She was touched by the generosity of the porters who carried the rice and India meal to
the vessels for shipment to Ireland in the famine, refusing all payment; and she knit with
her own hands a woollen comforter for each porter, of bright and pretty colours, which
she sent to a friend to present to the men, who were proud and grateful for the gifts; but,
alas! before they received them, those kind hands were cold, and that warm heart had
ceased to beat.*

A Memoir of Maria Edgeworth by Frances Edgeworth

Anger. *Work.* Confusion—what is to be done?
—the Atlantic in the way and the news getting worse,
work stretching to occupy every hour in the day,
carrying back and forth, lifting bearing and setting down.

We are in the centuries when work told the body how
to lift, fasten and drag, the weight of the world needed heaving,
when the horses staggered and slowed on the steep hill
the coach too full, too heavy to drag onwards—

they stopped fearfully and the child from the cabin
was waiting for his chance, he ran out with a stone,
pushed it behind the wheel so the horses could breathe
and waited for the farthings flung from the passengers' windows.

Now he is carrying sacks of meal to the boat
back and forth, loaded then free, and the work stretching ahead
like the road where at the same moment Maria Edgeworth
walks out, her young servant beside her carrying

the basket that gets a bit lighter
at every cabin door. This is her work now
at the end of her life. At home,
she sits down to the story she is writing,

line after line, her hand straying back and forth
across her remaining pages. The child from the cabin
is a man carrying meal to the docks, and at last
the day is over, and time for him to be paid—

but he is too angry, his colleagues are too angry
to take money for helping to feed starving people. And she
who is not ever recorded as being angry
takes out her knitting needles and the long skeins of wool

the women have spun in the cabins, to make
a warm comforter for every man, her needles
twitching back and forth until the work is done.
She is famous and fortunate, she will be remembered.

Like the girl whose brothers were turned into swans,
she does what she knows, the long scarves piling
softly beside her chair, one after the other like the days.

The men are far from home when her gift reaches them, the trace
of their work unraveling like a worn thread of wool, their kindness
out of anger stretched out across the Atlantic, for an answer.

THE FACES

1. Woman in a Traffic Jam

I still see the woman, a drowned
face rising up out of a wave,
time combing back strands of her hair.

I see her now just as clearly
as when we traveled beside her;
the man was raging at the wheel

as in forty minutes we moved
and paused again in jammed traffic;
she had her knitting out, her face

never altered. A mile ahead
some disaster made a headline;
sometimes we inched forward, sometimes

they slid ahead by a few yards.
It was like history, held there
in view of another lifetime:

we climbed the cogged wheel of our age,
our century, side by slow side.

2. *The Cobbler of Spilimbergo*

So through a thickened lens of time
I see clear over centuries
Domenico the cobbler,
his face a metaphor, like her

actual face, held still. He owned
these three books: *The Decameron,*
Orlando Furioso, and

a vernacular *Testament*,
and when the inquisitors came
and confiscated all of them

he swore *I'll never read again.*
I see his eyes, they are searching
for words vanished, the wave of time

sweeping over him with headlines
he cannot read, gripped in traffic,
his fate redacted, his eyes blank.

THE BOOKSHELVES

These are our cliffs, where we hang and grope and slide.
Why should there be a path upwards among such casual
stacks? Somebody shelved them size by size
but still they signal throbbing on shadow types.
Their lightning blazes like a faraway headlight
bound firmly elsewhere. Most times
it's the finger tucked in the big dictionary that leads
onward (as if under submerged voussoirs, along
damp paving to the ancient reservoir) to tell us
that the jumping flashes on the rockface were the codes
for a name that we could never have otherwise known.

MONSTERS

Now that there's nothing I don't understand,
why do they come to me with their informations?
They come in my dreams with their highlighting pens,
they tell me the roman numerals
on the shelf-end panels in the cathedral library
have all been regilded, someone has worked
with agate and crows' feathers to raise
gold flourishes and leaf script capitals. Show us,
they ask, the book that opens like a curtain;
and I tell them about the day I met
Ovid in the street, and he passed me
without a greeting.
              He had just thought
of the words that made the shrouds and tackling
swell with small buds, then looping stems,
then five-pointed leaves of ivy
catching, clutching the oars.

When I read it again myself I can see the oarsmen
frozen at their work, the sleepy drunk youngster
they were planning to sell, that wept
when they tied his hands, all of a sudden in charge,
his forehead ornate with grapes—

he is balanced on delicate sandals,
watching how they change, their spines
curve, they dance in the waves, each man
a monster to his neighbor.

THE CAPTURE

i

First, I need help to make the frame, with wings
and a nose and a tail fin,
room for those thick-furred beasts
if they scramble up or settle out of the air,
and a crack to harbor seeds for a trail of leaves,

so when I leap away the horizon swings
in the far distance, the hills
are floating like smoke, the fields
and the valley exposed then diving, the plane
flashing, and in every hollow under the leaves

a life huddles listening for a note that stings
music into life, a song that jumps that grieves.

ii

Except that I am not the earth but a late map of this earth,
its hedges tacking me down, don't expect me
to race again. The yearly bands of children

at school under the hedges are memorizing
their alphabets and fluxions and the distances
grow longer with every name called on the roll.

I could eclipse and cloud them with a wink
as there's no room left in the passages of my brain
for every conversation between the slug and the leaf,

yet if I follow the slow air where it spreads tracking
the laboring boats across the oceans,
where it knocks at every door and pushes inside,
where it winds along roads in France beside
the daughters leaving home to serve strangers,
the sons in foreign fields, the one holding
King Louis' hand on the scaffold as he prays,
the earth recedes.

 Can they all be crammed and keyed, "the Irish race
through history," which terms do we lack, to hold
that frame together, and how can we see anything
without the frame?
                        If I am a screen flickering
between the four handpainted provinces
and the bricks and timber,
this roof that shelters me,

I should find the bits of the frame,

I should walk around them to see if

they could be matched awry, to a different plan,

then try if I can persuade them

to limp back over the hedges, and

if then I'll feel the weight of the beasts

as they settle again along the mismatched wings.

SPACE

She has looked for a space, empty so she can grow,
and three dimensions seemed enough. The room
contains her, the white ceramic tiles visible
beyond the archway, where the low door thrown open
swings: all is void, and the packed stuff
menacing her for months in toppling stacks
is cleared and abandoned

                          —just

then without warning
down on the river
the ship that lay moored
for three whole days, its
temporary lights,
empty decks shining,
begins its journey
again, silently,
stiffly almost, down
to where the river
spreads wide and smooth
open to the tides
and slips off—smaller—
out on the channel.

VIEW

Now the traffic pauses, *now,*
help me to climb on the table,
then a leg up to the windowsill,
and then I'll turn, my right knee
cold against the copper pipes,
to get a view. If anyone looks
they can see the tear in my stocking,
but the view—

                right into the room
through to the alcove where the portrait
used to hang. Such a long time,
and when the wind stops blowing
the curtain across I can see
the shape on the wall. It's a line of dust
against the pale blue-green.

At least that's real; the portrait is gone.
It was a woman, the eyes
clearly reflecting a shrunken image,
Saint Sebastian, seized,
bound, for a martyr. Once he occupied
the whole wall, the tall space

behind the high altar—

                  now

when I look into her eyes I see him,

the ruined pillar, the antique stones,

his elegant writing body and

her eager eyes making him shrink

as the dusty line

calls me to view her, *now*, on the shadowed

pale blue-green wall.

SEAWEED

FOR THOMAS DILLON AND GERALDINE PLUNKETT,

MARRIED APRIL 23RD 1916

Everything in the room got in her way,
the table mirror catching the smoke
and the edges of the smashed windowpanes.
Her angle downward on the scene
gave her a view of hats and scattered stones.
She saw her brother come out to help
with the barricades, the wrecked tram
blocking off Earl Street, then back inside.

And for the man in the room, obscured
by her shadow against the window
the darkening was a storm shifting his life—
he wondered, where were they now, and would
this perch above the scene blow apart soon,
and he imagined the weeds that sink their filaments
between rocks to nourish a life in water
until all of a sudden they're sheared away to sea.

And out at sea the gunboat was bucking and plunging,
throwing up spray. The weeds are slapped

back again on sharp rocks beside beaches
that are sucked bare by the storm after this one,
their holdfast plucked away. He was thinking,
would they find a place and lose it, blown away
again, and find another, on the western coast,
as the seaweed is landed, a darkness in the dark water.

THE RAGING FOAM

FOR LELAND BARDWELL (FEBRUARY 1922–JUNE 2016)

i

Everything is late after an awful spring,
the morning sun, floating among clouds
when it ought to be shining between those two tall trees,
the fresh blue flower that should be here
to catch the light, making the minute real,
not open yet: they miss their yearly meeting.
I hear the news of her death and I wonder,
the seat behind her house that was a suntrap,
right by the sea, the waves
splashing and foaming on the rocks below,
is the sun late there, is there only shade?

ii

The foam breaks and withdraws.
It's a scatter of moments remembered,
my life, her life; and I gather them all up,
old scenes that are broken rumors

thrown high by the waves

(the horses swimming to the pier,

the baby in her cradle tossed

into the waiting currach). A segment

I recognize, the foam,

soapy water under a boat's side;

and looking down now in the profound

bay of memory, trying to guess how deep,

I see her in a ladylike tweed coat placing

black spectacles to read in a clear

ladylike voice, the night Patrick Kavanagh died:

Walk on serenely, do not mind

That Promised Land you thought to find . . .

iii

I know the date Kavanagh died, I know the date

in two thousand and thirteen we lost her

on the train to Cork and found her again on the station

walking on serenely accompanied

by the remote jingling of the keys

of all her houses, the voices of all the strays

remembering the floors they slept on,

the unhooking in the small hours.

iv

And even in the late nights
when the house was full already,
they dragged it out, the *Raging Foam*
for the last of the latchicoes with no home to go to.

v

The wild girl in Leixlip, the mother in London,
her children dancing half-naked in summer
on Karl Marx's grave, the woman I rode out with
in the Phoenix Park on the little polo ponies,
which was later than some places and before so many others—
I remember, or she told me, or someone had the story,
but as the sea rises up to flood the pools between rocks
making one shining surface of rising water
where all the reflected lights floating shine together,
they carry the glint of all the colors,
the headstalls of horses, the written pages and her face:
they are there with scraps and overnight guests and children
claiming, allowing no precedence, only the black cat
crouches on its dry shelf of time, the last of a dynasty of kittens.

A SLOW MARCH

Lento, as a threshold wearing down,
as the hesitant writer's hand,
the man with the trombone
stands waiting for the moment, for
the horn solo to finish, for the pause
until he lifts the long slider.

No other tone brings the body
so close, and how does it speak
about distance too? declaring the presence
of a breathing body, the note steady
as the lungs are slowly pushing out air
and the sound travels for miles,

while the girl with the piccolo is still
waiting her turn, for her five bars,
watching while he plays, her stance
as stiff as the pins holding her hair
flattened in place, gripping it down—
one eye on the score, counting the repeats.

And what harm if these characters
were to wear down to a trace and be lost

like the bump of an old defensive wall?
It would still take longer than
the notes of the trombone
and the piccolo too, fading away.

FASTNET

The winds go past, and the waves,
they forget where they were aiming
like a mind whose door is blown open
by another life imagined,
If only, forgetting the present:
O, any time, not now, anywhere
but not here, and the storm
sticks to us, a tall shadow marching
beside us, big as a darkening cloud—

no way of slowing down,
another life compelling,
and the wind is a Gothic parade
with faces like Castlereagh
seven bloodhounds beside him
panting for wider carnage,
faces that zoom and then pull back
and each of the serial lives is
plunged and then dragged to the surface.

Only the man that minds the light,
watching the great revolving spokes
hitting the piled castles of spray,

can say, trapped, not able to save,
This is life, I am living it now,
here, and the rock answers him back
as they wait for the storm to change its key,
It is yours, yours alone, you are living it here.

AN INFORMANT

When I asked her about the fate of the mission ship
sent away so many years ago
(and we knew then they'd be lucky to make land),
I could see she knew. She couldn't stop talking,
but her words sounded foreign.
I heard her sigh at last, taking off her gloves,
then silently picking up one of the lamps,
and she moved to the front door.
It was stiff, it hadn't been opened
since the last visit of the Vicar Forane,
but we found the key and pulled it wide.
She laid the lamp down in the doorway
and looked along the broad walk, to the gate
that is a roofed arch, with an alcove
intended for laying down a coffin,
so the bearers could take a rest. Sighing,
lifting the lamp, she carried it down there,
and I understood the words she used,
and what she wanted, for the action
to be complete. That we would leave it
there in the archway until the oil was spent
and the lamp died of its own accord.

The flame that had flickered pale in the daylight
shone steadily in the deep shade of the arch.
This is the short form, she said, we must
do this at least. This much we owe their names.

HOFSTETTER'S SERENADE

(MÁIRE NÍ CHUILLEANÁIN, 1944–1990)

I felt the draft just now as I was keying in the numbers—
the date of her death, going on twenty-five years ago;
it is May but the bright evening is turning colder,
the tight bundle of grief has opened out and spread
wide across these years she knows nothing of, and if I go
in search of her I must unwind and stretch out the thread
she left us, so it twines like a long devious border
turning between the music stands, over and under
the kettledrums and the big bass lying on its side;
but it plunges away leaving the concert-hall behind
and catches her at the start, in the year she was eleven, when
it first rose out of her, the pure line of sound that grows
rising dipping never landing twice on the same spot, then
catching its breath and then flowing along as even
as her own breathing, smooth like a weaver's thread
back and forth tracing. It weaves and it hops again,
the arched finger nails down the note but it overflows.

She was eleven years old. A thousand years before,
she could have been married to an emperor, she was sure
she was able to consent on the spot, as the notes wrapped around her, and

she went on playing as her eyes opened. Like words,
like the long serpent that can only swim upstream, like time,
the line drew her along, the string and the bow, towards
the moment I saw the breath leaving her body, and the silence began.

THE MORANDI BRIDGE

Let me lean my cheek against this limestone pillar—
I want to press until I feel the buzzing,
the sound the world makes when it isn't going
anywhere, a purr of gray transparent wings

hovering in one place. A humming to itself
because it needs to lie still, stay quiet and
recover, and who will bring help?
                                        The noise
when the bridge fell down in Genova—the road

you and I drove along slowly, heading east
behind a small Fiat, packed and weighed down
with people, cake and flowers for a mother-in-law
that made a Sunday lunch; they were taking their time—

it was lunchtime again each year when we reached the bridge,
and the families were always on the move,
so we'd drive along slowly, those fifteen minutes
high up over the factories and streets—

I would tell you this news if the stones of the world
could carry language, but after eight months, the shock
and the noise inside them still, they cannot move
or even allow a message to pass through.

APRIL 2019

AG STÁNADH AMACH

Agus í ag stánadh amach, ina seasamh san áit sin, ag stánadh ag féachaint amach trí fhuinneóg ard thuas staighre. An staighre ard deas caol, agus cairpéad uaithne air. Agus cad a chonaic sí ach slua mór daoine, ach nárbh fhéidir léi iad a fheiscint go cruinn soiléir mar gheall ar an sneachta a bhí ag titim le fada.

Cén fáth gur tháinig na focail sin ar ais chuici, focail na mná feasa?

Fear agus ualach mór á iompar aige go tuathalach, bean á leanúint, páiste ar a droim agus páiste eile ina láimh aici, cailín óg ag rith lena cois. Seandaoine ag luí siar fágtha ar deireadh. Agus an sneachta ag titim anuas gan stad, ag súrac gach imire óna mbalcaisí, iad ag cosaint a gceann is a n-aghaidh ar an ngaoth chomh maith agus ab fhéidir leo, ionas nach n-aithneofaí iad.

Aon bhábóg amháin ina láimh ag cailín beag, gúna bán uirthi agus ribín dearg. Cén fáth gur thugadar ribín dearg di, an tuar fola é sin?

Na daoine ag triall thart gan cabhair a fháil ó éinne, agus an oíche ag luathú. Iad beagnach dofheicthe ach bhí a fhios aici go rabhadar ann fós agus slua eile á leanúint. D'fhan sí ag an bhfuinneog go dtí gur éirigh an ghealach agus chonaic sí an taobh tíre: folamh, bán, sleamhain snasta. Bhí an ghaoth ina tost agus mar sin chuala sí na saighdiúirí i bhfad sar a thángadar i láthair. Fuaim na leoraithe i bhfad, ag brostú ar an áit, ag brostú i dtreo di.

Ach níor leagadar láimh uirthi, bhí sí socair sábháilte thuas staighre. Fiú níor tharraing sí an cuirtín, níor mhúch an solas. D'fhan sí ann agus a gúna corcra agus an cairpéad uaithne ag lonrú amach. Nuair a

GAZING OUT

As she gazed out, standing upright in that place, gazing looking out of a high upstairs window. Fine high narrow stairs, a green carpet. Then what did she see only a great host of people, only that she could not see them clearly because of the snow that had been falling for ages.

Why did the words come back to her, the words of the wise woman?

A man awkwardly carrying a big bundle, a woman following him, a child on her back and another held by the hand, a young girl running at her side. Old people at the back, left behind. The snow ceaselessly falling, leaching every tinge from their old clothes, they shielded their heads and their faces as well as they could against the wind, in the hope of not being recognized.

A little girl holding a single doll, a white dress on her, a red ribbon. Why did they give her a red ribbon, does that stand for blood?

The people passing along without help from anyone, night coming on. Almost invisible but she knew they were still there and another host following them. She stayed at the window until the moon rose and she saw the countryside empty, white, smooth, clean. The wind had fallen silent and so she heard the soldiers long before they came. Noise of lorries far away, hurrying to the place, hurrying towards her.

But they did not lay a hand on her, she was safe and sound upstairs. She did not draw the curtain or put out the light. She stayed there, her purple dress and the green carpet shining out. When they were gone they

d'imigh siad d'fhágadar a rian ar an sneachta, agus ansan do thosnaigh an sneachta arís agus chlúdaigh an lorg.

Cén fáth gur tháinig focail na mná sin ar ais chuici? *At chíu forderg, at chíu rúad.* Nuair a tháinig Fedelm chun eolas a thabhairt don bhanríon faoi na rudaí a bhí le teacht, labhair sí as a carbad, is d'éist an bhanríon ina carbad féin. Ar an leibhéal céanna. Iad gléasta mar an gcéanna, éadaí ildathacha orthu araon. Ach mise, dúirt sí ina haigne féin, anseo mar atáim, socair sábháilte thuas staighre, ní fheicim ach an méid atá os mo chomhair, san aimsir láithreach. Nach leor san d'aon duine amháin?

Loinnir frithchaite ón sneachta á soilsiú.

left their track on the snow, and then it started to snow again and covered the traces.

Why did that woman's words come back to her? *I see them crimson, I see them red.* When Fedelm came to tell the queen what she foresaw, she spoke from her chariot, and the queen listened from her own chariot. On the same level. They were dressed similarly. Both dressed in many colors. But, said she to herself in her own mind, from this place I'm in, safe and sound, I can only see what is in front of me, in the present. Is that not enough for a single person?

The reflected light from the snow shining on her.

AN CRANN

An teach a d'fhágamar i naoi déag dathad is a naoi
—Agus gan fhios ag éinne fós cé mhéad páiste
Atá tar éis fás suas ins an áit chéanna ó shin
—Maireann an crann a chuir m'athair ann,
Ach cad a tharla don gcasán soiminte a leag seisean,
Rud a theaspáin dom conas a thriomaíonn an tsoimint fén ngaoth?
Is ann a d'fhoghlamas conas mar a bhíonn an saol
Idir mhnáibh is fearaibh, mo mháthair sa bhaile linne,
M'athair ag teacht abhaile, ise ag fiafraí as Gaeilge,
"Bhfuil aon scéal agat?"
An cailín aimsire sa chistin, sneachta i mí na Nollag,

Go dtí go bhfuaireas amach nach raibh an méad sin
Ceart in aon chor. Chuamar go léir ar aghaidh
Ar bhealach éigin eile, á leanúint
Mar a fhásann an crann, gach géag ag nochtadh a léarscáil féin,
Go dtí an lá go dtáinig an áit ar ais chugam
Agus d'fhanas go dtiocfadh na focail, thosnaíos á dtóraíocht
Ar leibhéal níos doimhne fós, díreach mar a chuardaíonn an phréamh
A bealach fé thalamh, ag lorg cothaithe is buntobair.

THE TREE

The house we left in 1949
—and who knows now how many children
have grown up in that same place since then
—the tree is alive that my father planted there.
But what happened to the cement path he laid,
that showed me how cement dries under the wind?
That's where I learned how the world is
between men and women, my mother with us at home,
my father coming home, her asking him in Irish
"Have you any news?"
the maid in the kitchen, snow in December,

until I found out that all that information
wasn't true at all. We moved on
along a different road, that we followed
as the tree grows, every branch displaying a map of its own,
until the day the place came back to me
and I waited for the words to come, I began searching
in a still deeper seam, just as the root explores
its road underground, looking for sustenance and a source.

ACKNOWLEDGMENTS

Acknowledgments are due to the editors of the following publications where some of these poems, or versions of them, were published first: *Angle*, *Café Review*, *Clifden 35*, *College Green*, *Eavan Boland: Inside History* (Arlen House 2017), *The Enchanting Verses Literary Review*, *Famine Folios: Leaves of Hungry Grass: Poetry and Ireland's Great Hunger* (Cork University Press 2016), *fermata: Poems inspired by Music* (eds. Vincent Woods and Eva Bourke), *gorse*, *Irish-Italian Studies: New Perspectives on Cultural Mobility and Permeability* (ed. Chiara Sciarrino, Palermo University Press 2018), *The Irish Times*, *Migrant Shores* (Salmon Poetry 2017), *Reading the Future: New Writing from Ireland* (Arlen House/Hodges Figgis 2018), *Southword*, *Strokestown Poetry Anthology* (2017 and 2018), and *Unde Scribitur* (Amergin Solstice Gathering, 2018).

"An Imperfect Enclosure" was published by the Nano Nagle Centre in Cork. Several of these poems appeared in *Hofstetter's Serenade* (Periplum 2016).

"For James Connolly" was commissioned by the Irish Writers' Centre for the film *A Poet's Rising* and published in an accompanying pamphlet.

"View" was published in a limited signed edition for Friends of The Gallery Press.